A to Z Treasures:

Learning Through Bible Poetry

by
Sandra A. McTiernan
& Leila Rose-Gordon

Illustrated by Sandra A. McTiernan
Edited by Leila Rose-Gordon
& Sandra A. McTiernan

A to Z Treasures:

Learning Through Bible Poetry

By Sandra A. McTiernan
& Leila Rose-Gordon

Publisher's Cataloging-in-Publication data

Names: McTiernan, Sandra A., author. | Rose-Gordon, Leila, author.
Title: A to Z treasures : learning through Bible poetry / by Sandra A. McTiernan & Leila Rose-Gordon ; illustrated by Sandra A. McTiernan; edited by Leila Rose-Gordon & Sandra McTiernan.
Description: Queens, NY: Stirring Hearts Publishing, 2020. | Summary: Let us take you on an A to Z journey through Bible stories! Learn the alphabet and the Bible at the same time.
Identifiers: LCCN: 2021922863 | ISBN: 978-1-7379551-0-8
Subjects: LCSH Bible stories, English. | English language--Alphabet--Juvenile literature. | BISAC JUVENILE NONFICTION / Religion / Bible Stories / General | JUVENILE NONFICTION / Concepts / Alphabet
Classification: LCC BS551.3 .M38 At 2021 | DDC 235/.3--dc23

This book is dedicated to Jesus Christ
and
all the beautiful children
of the world!

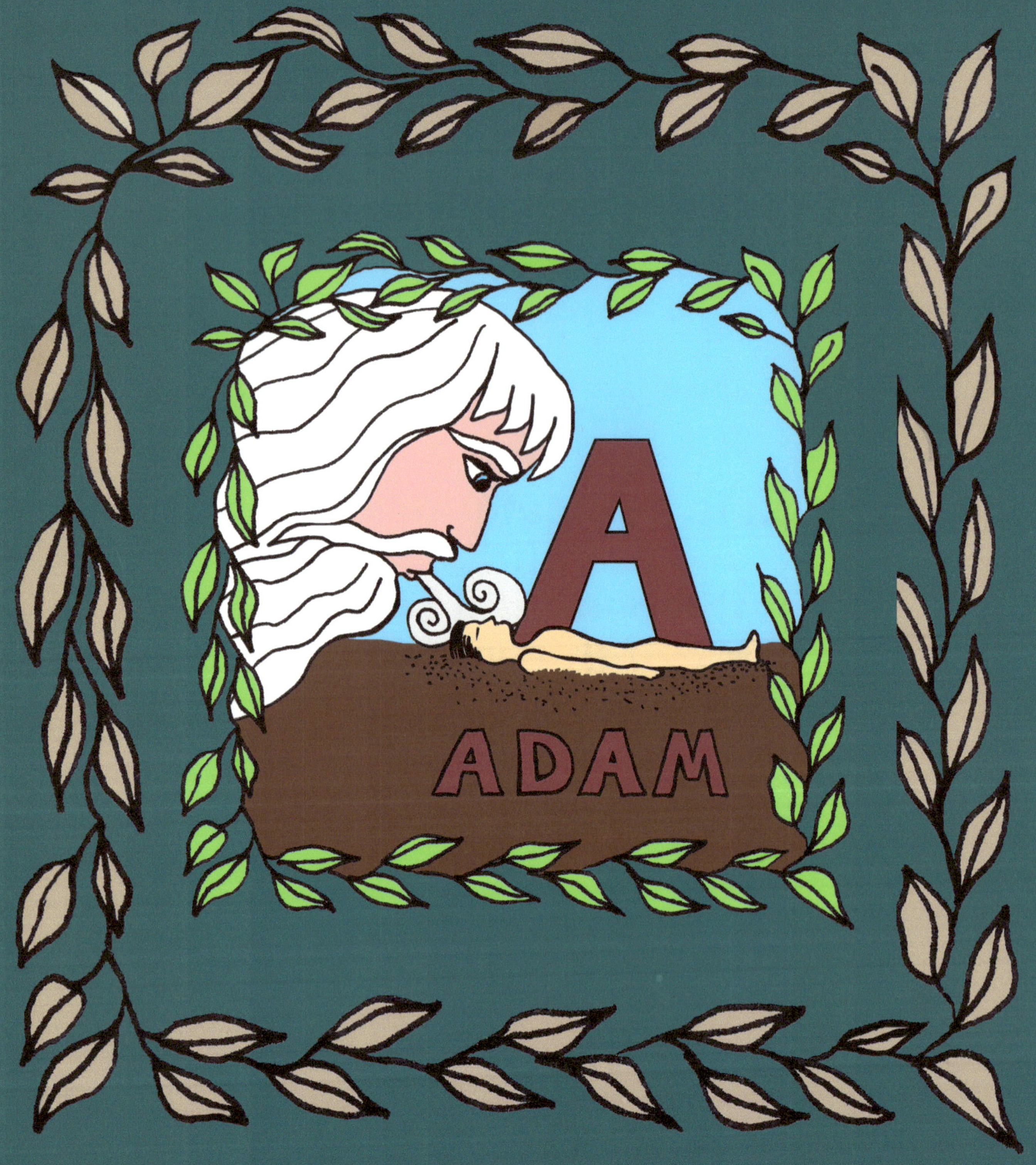
A
ADAM

A for **Adam**, the very first man,
formed by God from the dust of the land.
God breathed in him the breath of life,
and gave him Eve to be his wife.

B
BIBLE

B is for **Bible**. It is God’s word,
to tell God’s love ‘til everyone’s heard.
It tells too of how the world began,
and of all God’s help He gave to man.

COMMANDMENTS

C is for Commandments. God gave us ten,
To know and love Him and our fellowmen.
Rules help us to know just what to do.
God, may Your laws make me be like You.

D
DANIEL

D is for Daniel, cast in the lion's den,
Because he prayed to God and not unto men.
Daniel surely, God did save.
Lord, help me to be as brave!

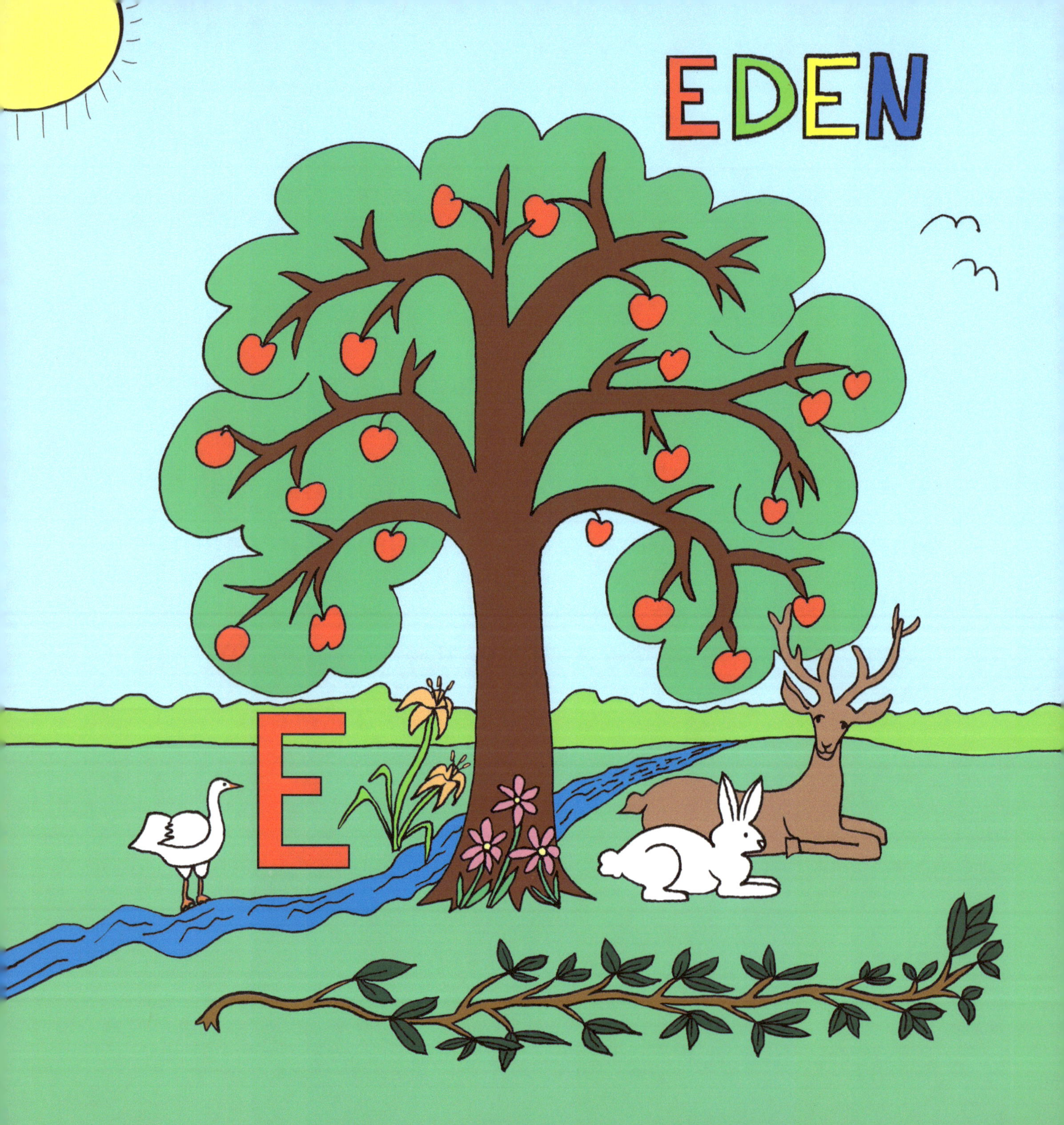
EDEN
E

E is for **Eden**, home of Adam and Eve:
A garden so pretty you won't want to leave.
Filled with lovely animals and beautiful trees;
It has babbling brooks and a sweet, gentle breeze.

F
FISHERMEN

F is for **Fishermen** trying hard to catch fish.
None came in their nets, however hard they did wish.
When Jesus made fish in the nets overflow,
they left all for Him, with their faces aglow.

GOD
G

G is for **God**, in a guiding white cloud by day;
for Moses and his crowd, this cloud led the way.
A pillar of fire by night, God cast a sweet light,
to give Moses and his people clear sight.

H
HEAVEN

H is for **Heaven** where God has His home.
Jesus is with Him, seated on His great throne.
We know Jesus will return for us one day.
Let's get ready and let's show others the way!

I
INFANT

I is for **Infant**, so tender and mild;.
Jesus once was a little Child.
Born to Mary and Joseph who lived here on Earth,
but knew that their Child was of heavenly birth.

J
JONAH

J is for **Jonah**, swallowed by a big fish.
He prayed to God who granted his wish.
God led the fish to burp him ashore,
then he gladly spread God's message galore.

K
IS
FOR
KING

K is for **King**, and there is only One:
The Father, the Spirit, and the Son.
They're one in mind and also in heart...
They can work together or apart.

L
LOVE

L is for the precious Love of God
that falls on me from heaven above...
It warms my heart like rays of sun,
and helps us all to be as one.

M
MIGHTY!

M is for **Mighty**. Goliath's steps shook the ground.
Every soldier he challenged shook with fear at the sound!
But God gave great courage to David, a lad,
who killed Goliath with a sling and made the people glad.

N
IS
FOR
NAAMAN

N is for **Naaman**, a leper, who longed to be whole.
Captain of an army, he was a mighty soul.
He learned about a man of God who told him what to do.
And when he followed all those words, his skin became brand new!

O
OBEY
1 2 3 4
5 6 7 8 9 10

O is for **Obey**: Try to follow God's way.
Listen to your parents, and do what they say.
Keep the Ten Commandments as a guide for you.
We show we love God by the things that we do!

P
PRAYER

P is for **Prayer** to God, our Creator.
He hears us and answers us, now or later.
You may not hear His voice as a sound,
but in quiet God's will can be found.

QUIET
Q

Q is for **Quiet**, a good time for prayer.
You speak to God, for He's always there.
Be patient and wait, for His answers are sure!
He'll do what is best for your life evermore.

LAZARUS, COME FORTH!!
R
RAISE

R is for Raise; Jesus woke Lazarus from death.
He heard Jesus' voice and then took a new breath.
Saints will rise when Jesus comes again.
The day He returns, we know not when.

S IS FOR SERVE
TEACH
ABC
HELP
FEED
SEW
BUILD
MAKE
COOK
CLEAN
FIX

S is for **Serve**: taking care of the needs of others.

This includes mothers, fathers, sisters, and brothers.

For Jesus healed sick, hurt and blind;

In every way, Jesus was kind to mankind!

T
TIMOTHY

T is for **Timothy**; he was a young lad,
with great faith like his grandma and mom had.
He became a great teacher with Silas and Paul,
and sailed away from his country to heed God's call.

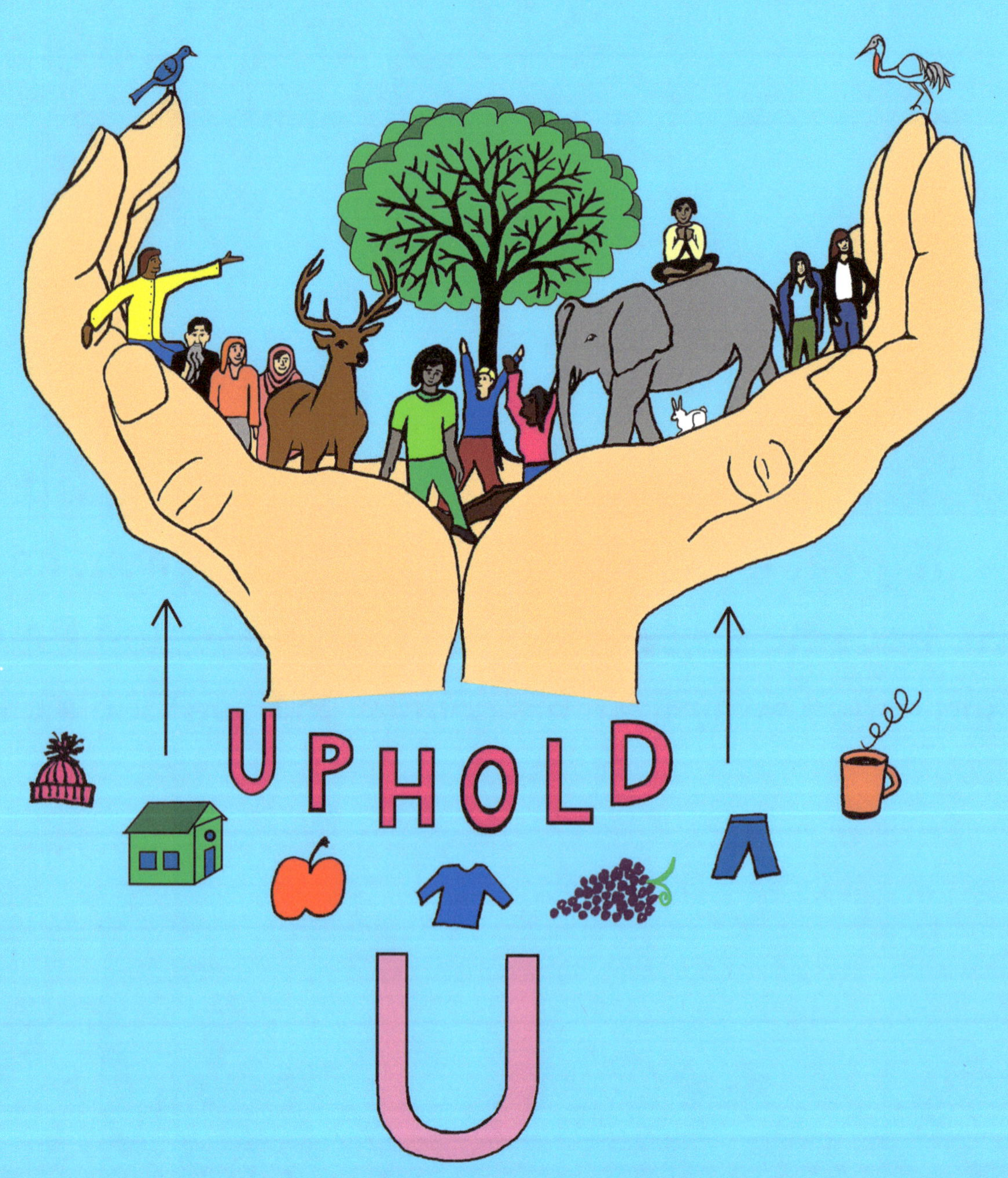
UPHOLD
U

U is for Uphold; God supports us all;
from creation and even after man's fall.
He takes care of creatures of earth, sea, and sky;
food, clothing, and shelter in abundant supply!

V
VICTORY

V is for **Victory** won by Jesus Christ:
God overcame evil at a terrible price.
Jesus came and died on a cruel cross,
So that all who accept Him will never be lost.

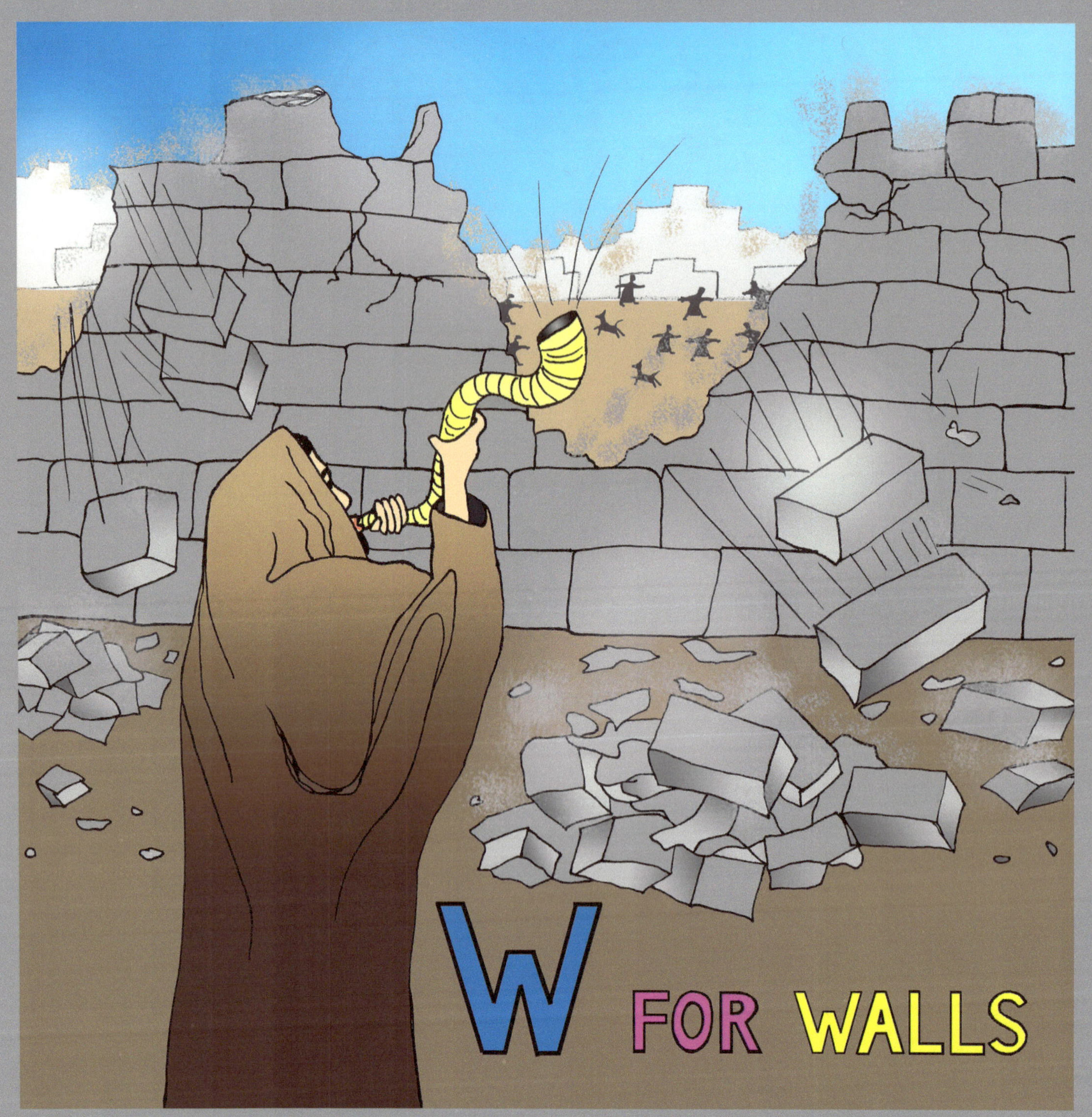
W FOR WALLS

W is for **Walls**--Jericho City's walls fell down when they marched the 7th day, 7 times around. The walls fell down fast at the trumpet's blast, and Jericho was defeated at last!

X

Sara & Kara

Carlos

Carlos

Xerox

X is for **Xerox**, exactly the same.
Some people look alike; some have the same name.
But if you look closely, you surely will find:
God makes us all special and one-of-a-kind!

YET
Y

Y is for **Yet**; for our God is not done.
He's working on us; but the victory's won!
Yes; we shall be perfect in robes clean and white,
but now we're still learning about wrong and right.

Z
ZACCHAEUS

Z is for **Zaccheus**, a wee tax taker
Who accepted Jesus as his true Maker.
He climbed up a tree to get Jesus in sight;
Jesus looked up and said, “Let’s have dinner tonight!”

About the Authors

Sandra A. McTiernan is a writer, artist/graphic designer, singer, teacher, and school nurse. She lives in Ridgewood, New York. Sandra holds a BFA from Long Island University in Southampton, but is self-taught with regard to graphic arts. She worked three years as a special education teacher, and currently as a school nurse. She teaches the Bible to children weekly.

Sandra has been friends with co-author Leila Rose-Gordon ever since coming to Mount Moriah SDA Church. The partnership has been a delight for both!

Sandra likes to illustrate by hand first before editing and colorizing in Adobe Photoshop. To see more of her work and hear her tell Bible stories, please visit:

Sandra can be emailed at sandymct@hotmail.com.

About the Authors:

Leila Rose-Gordon

loves God and daily responds with gratitude to her higher calling. She lives in New York with her husband, John Gordon (a mathematics lecturer), and their son, Jeremy, who is author of two books: *The Boy Who Loves Rules* and *A Ray of Hope.*

Leila is an attorney working in the Legal Department at the Northeastern Conference of Seventh-day Adventists. Leila has a master's in reading and literacy from Capella University.

Leila is author of *Children's Picture Book of Animal Poems, Forgiveness Poetry Journal,* and the devotional *Beside Still Waters.*

There is a narrated video of this book Copyright 2020 on youtube under Sandra McTiernan:

https://youtu.be/vSJC3qy6pcs

www.ingramcontent.com/pod-product-compliance
Lightning Source LLC
LaVergne TN
LVHW070149110826
845147LV00002B/356

* 9 7 8 1 7 3 7 9 5 5 1 0 8 *